Harvest Mouse

by Oxford Scientific Films

**Photographs by George Bernard,
Sean Morris and David Thompson**

G. P. Putnam's Sons New York

First American edition 1982
Text copyright © 1981 by Jennifer Coldrey
Photographs copyright © 1981 by Oxford Scientific Films
Ltd.
All rights reserved.
Printed in Belgium by Henri Proost & CIE PUBA
Library of Congress Cataloging in Publication Data
Main entry under title:
Harvest mouse.
Summary: Examines, in text and photographs, the life
and habits of the tiny European harvest mouse.
1. Micromys minutus—Juvenile literature.
[1. Harvest mouse, European. 2. Mice]
I. Oxford Scientific Films. II. Bernard, George, 1949–ill.
III. Morris, Sean, ill. IV. Thompson, David, 1945–ill.
QL737.R666H36   599.32'33   81-10685 AACR2
ISBN 0-399-20851-8
First impression.

In writing the introduction to this book reference was made by the author to the following titles by Stephen Harris: *Secret Life of the Harvest Mouse* (Hamlyn) and *The Harvest Mouse* (Blandford Press).

Harvest Mouse

The harvest mouse (*Micromys minutus*) is one of the smallest mammals in Europe. A fully grown adult weighs only one-fifth to one-third of an ounce, and its body is not much longer than a matchbox. Harvest mice are closely related to other mice and rats and belong to a large group of animals called Rodents. They are found in most European countries from the Mediterranean to the Arctic Circle and also right across Asia as far as Japan and the Pacific coast.

The harvest mouse has a blunt, rounded nose, and small hairy ears rather like a vole's. Long, stiff whiskers, which are very sensitive to touch, grow out of its upper lip. The tail is as long as the head and body together (about one and a half inches) and is used a great deal when climbing. The adult is russet-brown on the back and white on the underparts. This coloring explains why the animal is sometimes known as the "Red Mouse" or "Red Ranny." The harvest mouse has bright, black little eyes, but relies much more on its sensitive hearing to detect danger. It will react to strange noises or vibrations by first freezing in place and then stealing away through the vegetation to safety.

Harvest mice can be quarrelsome and aggressive, especially in late winter and early spring when they are hungry and competing for food. When fighting, they face each other on their hind legs, snarling and showing their teeth and boxing each other with their forefeet. They attack and bite off pieces of the tail and will even kill and eat each other if conditions are very severe.

Like all Rodents, harvest mice have two front gnawing teeth (incisors), typical of vegetarian feeders, although they also eat insects, which are an important part of the diet as they provide extra protein. Harvest mice have been seen catching and feeding on butterflies, moths, caterpillars, ladybugs and other beetles.

Wild fruits and seeds of all kinds make up the greater part of their diet; seed and grain are particularly nutritious because of their high energy content. In early spring, when food is scarce, harvest mice eat young plant shoots. A little later in the year they have been seen sipping sweet nectar from cowslip flowers. In fall they enjoy juicy blackberries and other ripe fruits.

Not many people are lucky enough to see harvest mice in the wild, because they are so tiny and secretive. They like to live in areas of tall thick vegetation, either in the long grass at the edge of a road, or in ditches, hedges, bramble patches, rushes and reed beds and even overgrown parts of the garden. One of their favorite haunts is the cornfield, where the combination of tall, strong, closely planted stalks and a plentiful supply of grain is ideal.

Harvest mice are small, light, agile and can swing and climb around on the stalks like miniature acrobats. They twist their tails around the stems and use the tip like an extra foot to grip and help them balance. When they climb down, the tail is used as a brake. The hind feet have specially adapted outer toes, rather like thumbs, which are also extremely useful for clinging on to grass or cereal stalks. The animal has an amazing sense of balance, and can hold on tightly with its tail and hind feet, leaving the small, sensitive forefeet free for feeding, washing and cleaning, fighting or even building a nest.

Harvest mice build several different types of nest, but they are all more or less round in shape and cleverly constructed from woven grass leaves. According to the type of grass, the nests may be built quite close to the ground, or as much as three feet above it. The young are commonly born in nests well above the ground, where they are safe from predators.

Small nests of loosely woven grass, measuring about one and a half inches in diameter, are often made as a temporary home for a mouse to shelter in. However, the nests used for breeding are larger than this (up to four inches in diameter), and are more carefully constructed with a soft inner lining of finely chewed grass.

A typical breeding nest is usually made by the female harvest mouse a few days before she is ready to give birth. She first bites the surrounding grass stems in several places to weaken them and so make it easier to bend them into position. Then, using her teeth and forefeet, she shreds some nearby grass leaves into several thin strips, being careful to leave the base of the leaves entire and still attached to their stems, so that they will not die. The shredded leaves are woven together to form the framework of the nest. The mouse works from inside, pulling more grass leaves in through the wall before shredding them to weave into the lining. The final woven basket is stuffed with finely chewed grass and maybe some thistledown or bird feathers, to make a soft bed for the babies. There is no definite opening, and the mice simply push their way in and out through the flexibly woven walls.

These green summer nests are attached to the surrounding plants and are made of living grass leaves, so they are barely visible during the breeding season. Later in the year when the young have left the nest, the grassy walls go a yellowish brown and the nest is more easily seen.

Breeding takes place throughout the summer, usually

between June and October, although it can extend into December if the weather is favorable. Courtship begins during April and May. The female gives off an attractive scent which the male likes. He chases after her through the vegetation, squeaking, chattering and sniffing vigorously as he follows her. The female is often unwilling to mate and usually runs away; later she may even turn on the male angrily. When ready to mate she is less aggressive and answers the male with a chattering sound. He pursues her down to the ground where mating usually takes place. The female then chases the male away, and he plays no part in nest-building or rearing the young, and never enters the breeding nest.

The young are born seventeen to nineteen days after mating, and there may be from three to eight babies in a litter. They are blind, deaf and totally hairless at birth, looking like miniature pink piglets. Each baby is only half an inch long and weighs less than one and a half ounces. Their tails are relatively short and their heads seem large. The tiny babies lie curled up together in a ball in the center of the nest and move very little. They make very few noises, presumably so as not to attract predators.

By the time they are five days old their backs are covered with short brown hair, and two days later a short white fur has started to grow on their undersides. The eyes are open by the ninth day, and at this stage the young mice are able to move around weakly inside the nest. All this time they have been suckled by the mother, but now they also start to take chewed-up food from her mouth.

At twelve days old they can move about confidently and will make short journeys outside the nest. They can now use their tails to balance and grip with and may eat any soft seeds and green stuff they find, as well as starting to drink water.

At fifteen days the tail is full length and the young become independent. The mother now abandons the nest and leaves the young ones to look after themselves. She is usually pregnant with her next litter at this stage and goes off to build another nest nearby. A female can become pregnant every twenty-one days and may produce several litters in one year.

The young mice stay near the nest for a few days and then wander off on their own. At this stage they are a grayish-brown or sandy color; they become the reddish brown of the adult only after they have molted. They are full-sized adults at four to five weeks, at which time they are able to mate and produce young of their own.

When the young first leave the nest they are in great danger of being attacked by predators, as they have not yet learned to respond quickly to danger signals. Harvest mice are too small to be the main food of any one animal, but because they are active by night as well as by day they attract many different predators. Weasels, stoats, foxes, birds of prey, toads and even other rodents may attack and kill them, especially in fall and winter when food is short. At such times they are a favorite food of the night-hunting barn owl.

Weasels have also been known to attack young harvest mice in the nest, and if the mother suspects that there is a dangerous predator in the area she will quickly move her youngsters to a nearby nest, carrying each baby, one by one, to its new home. Normally, however, there are very few deaths in the nest, since it is cleverly camouflaged, well protected against the weather, and built high above the ground.

A more serious cause of death among harvest mice is exposure to cold and wet. Because they are so small these animals have a relatively large surface area from which heat is lost rapidly. While in the nest they are protected from the cold by the woven walls, which trap pockets of air and keep the temperature inside reasonably warm. The breeding nests are also fairly waterproof and only a very heavy downpour can penetrate and harm the young. However, once they have left the nest they are exposed and can easily die by getting chilled after heavy rain. Sudden frosts and cold winds during fall and winter kill hundreds of harvest mice, and only a very small proportion of the population survives till the following spring. In captivity harvest mice can live for several years, but in the wild it is unlikely that they live longer than a year, and most survive only for a few weeks or maybe months.

As winter approaches, many harvest mice move from their summer habitat to a warmer and safer place. At this time of year the fields are bare and cold and the animals retreat to the shelter provided by hedges, rough grassy banks, or barns and outbuildings. Nests may be built deep in a hedge, in a hole in a wall, under logs or stones and sometimes in an abandoned bird's nest or a deserted underground burrow. During the winter the animals live almost entirely at ground level,

seeking protection from strong winds and driving rain. They do not hibernate, but in very cold weather may spend long periods of time curled up tightly in their winter nests. If they are lucky, their fall diet of fruits and seeds will have enabled them to produce a thick layer of fat under the skin which helps to retain their body heat.

Harvest mice sheltering in farm buildings or in haystacks may find food for the winter, but for most of these tiny mammals it is a struggle to survive until the warmer weather arrives and the spring shoots start to grow.

Unfortunately, now that combine harvesters and other mechanical reapers are commonly used on farms, there are fewer haystacks for mice to shelter in. The combine harvester, which cuts close to the ground, is a threat to harvest mice living in cornfields. Adults, and young which have recently left the nest, can leap to the ground and run for safety; but nests, and any newborn young in them, are almost certain to be squashed.

After the harvest, many farmers burn the stubble, an even worse horror to harvest mice still in the fields, since many get burned in the fire and those that survive are left unprotected and an easy prey for hungry predators. However, despite these and other manmade hazards, harvest mice still seem to thrive in the cereal crops which provide an ideal habitat for them. Because they are so tiny, harvest mice rarely eat enough corn to cause damage and they sometimes positively help the farmer by eating insect pests, such as wheat aphids.

Jennifer Coldrey

The tiny harvest mouse is not much bigger than the pull-tab from a can of soda.

A cornfield is a good place for climbing and finding grain to eat.

The harvest mouse is a marvelous acrobat. His light weight means he can jump from one slender stalk to another without breaking them.

He uses his long tail to help him balance, and also as a brake when climbing down stalks.

The outer toe on each back foot is used for gripping, like a thumb. The front feet, like hands, can gather and hold food.

The harvest mouse enjoys stealing the sweet nectar from the cowslip flower and the juice from a ripe blackberry in autumn.

Sometimes he catches and eats insects such as grasshoppers and butterflies.

When a male first courts a female she often turns on him in anger. Later, she lets him come nearer, and they investigate each other by sniffing.

After a chase through the grass, mating takes place on the ground.

The female begins her nest-building by shredding grass leaves and bending them between the stalks.

She weaves the leaves together to form the framework.

The finished nest is hard to see in the tall grass.

The babies are born inside the softly lined nest.

At first they look like tiny piglets. Their eyes and ears are closed.

The mother feeds the baby mice with her own milk.

After five days their backs are covered with dark fur, but their eyes and ears are not yet open.

These mice, about two weeks old and with their eyes open, are almost ready to leave the nest.

A young mouse is learning to climb, using its tail to grip the corn-stalks. It is much grayer than its mother.

A curious weasel means danger for a nest full of young.

The mother carries her baby mice to safety one by one.

This hungry toad is eating a harvest mouse he has just caught on the ground.

Crows normally feed on dead animals, but this one has caught a harvest mouse it spotted in the open.

Harvest mice will make a nest wherever there is thick plant cover. This one lives beside a busy road.

In the late summer the combine harvester threatens mice living in the cornfields.

The worst danger the harvest mouse has to face is the burning of stubble, and many tiny mice die in these fires. The mouse above has fled from the fire to the safety of a stream at the edge of the field.

Winter is a bad time for harvest mice. There is little food around and they cannot survive in the open in very cold weather.

These two have found shelter in an empty wren's nest.

The harvest mouse must keep his tail well groomed. Wherever he lives and whatever he is doing, he relies on this most useful limb.